HEAD-TO-TOE HEALTH

NOSEBLEEDS

ELAINE LANDAU

Marshall Cavendish
Benchmark
New York

Marshall Cavendish Benchmark
99 White Plains Road
Tarrytown, New York 10591
www.marshallcavendish.us

Expert Reader: Leslie L. Barton, M.D., professor emerita of Pediatrics,
University of Arizona College of Medicine, Tucson, Arizona

© 2010 Elaine Landau

All rights reserved.

No part of this book may be reproduced in any form without written permission from the copyright holders.

All Internet addresses were correct and accurate at the time of printing.

Library of Congress Cataloging-in-Publication Data
Landau, Elaine.
    Nosebleeds / by Elaine Landau.
        p. cm. — (Head-to-toe health)
    Includes bibliographical references and index.
    Summary: "Provides basic information about nosebleeds and their prevention"—Provided by publisher.
    ISBN 978-0-7614-3503-7
1. Nosebleeds—Juvenile literature. I. Title.
RF363.L36 2010
617.5'23—dc22   2008008057

Editor: Christine Florie
Publisher: Michelle Bisson
Art Director: Anahid Hamparian
Series Designer: Alex Ferrari

Photo research by Candlepants Incorporated

Cover photo by *Shutterstock*

The photographs in this book are used by permission and through the courtesy of:
Corbis: Tom Stewart, 4; Estelle Klawitter/zefa, 14; Norbert Schaefer, 19; JLP/Jose L. Pelaez, 22.
Photo Researchers Inc.: Mark Clarke, 5; J. Bavosi, 9. *Shutterstock*: 7. *SuperStock*: age fotostock, 8;
Kwame Zikomo, 12. *PhotoTakeUSA.com*: BSIP, 17, 21. *Getty Images*: Ken Chernus, 25.

Printed in Malaysia
1 3 5 6 4 2

CONTENTS

THERE GOES YOUR NOSE! . . . 5

KNOW YOUR NOSE . . . 7

NOSEBLEED! . . . 11

WHAT TO DO IF IT HAPPENS TO YOU . . . 15

KNOWING WHEN TO GET HELP . . . 19

GLOSSARY . . . 27

FIND OUT MORE . . . 28

INDEX . . . 30

There Goes Your Nose!

It's a beautiful spring day. You and your brother are at the park. You're playing catch and having a great time. Then suddenly, everything changes. Your brother pitches a ball that you don't catch. But it's worse than that. The ball hits you right in the face.

At first you feel a burning, stinging pain. Then, you look down at your shirt. There's blood on it. The blood is coming from your nose.

Your nose is bleeding, and you don't know what to do. You don't even

If your nose is injured and starts to bleed, don't worry. Most nosebleeds stop in a few minutes.

◀ Playing a game of catch is fun, but a missed ball can result in an injury or a nosebleed.

have a tissue with you. You feel really scared. You just hope you'll be okay.

NOSEBLEEDS HAPPEN

Having a nosebleed can be frightening. However, most nosebleeds aren't serious. They often look much worse than they are. Usually, nosebleeds can be stopped within minutes.

This book is all about nosebleeds. You'll learn what causes them as well as what to do to stop them. So if you want to become a junior nosebleed expert, read on!

> **DID YOU KNOW?**
> Nosebleeds are not rare. Nearly 60 percent of the people living in the United States will have nosebleeds sometime in their lives. Nosebleeds are most common among two groups: young children and elderly people.

Know Your Nose

You probably never think about your nose. It just sits on your face, below your eyes and above your mouth. Yet your nose is important. You use it every day to breathe. Your nose also allows you to smell. Noses come in different sizes and shapes. However, they all work in the same way.

INSIDE YOUR NOSE

From the outside your nose looks like it is one piece. But it actually has different parts. The two openings at the bottom of your nose are called nostrils. A thin wall called a **septum**

Everyone has a nose. Besides breathing, noses allow us to smell the world around us.

7

SUPERSNIFFERS

Question: Which do you think has a better sense of smell—a human or a dog?
Answer: Dogs can out smell people any day. Rescue workers often use dogs to pick up the scent of a missing person. Dogs have also been trained to sniff out drugs and bombs at docks and airports. Humans can't do that. A dog's nose really knows!

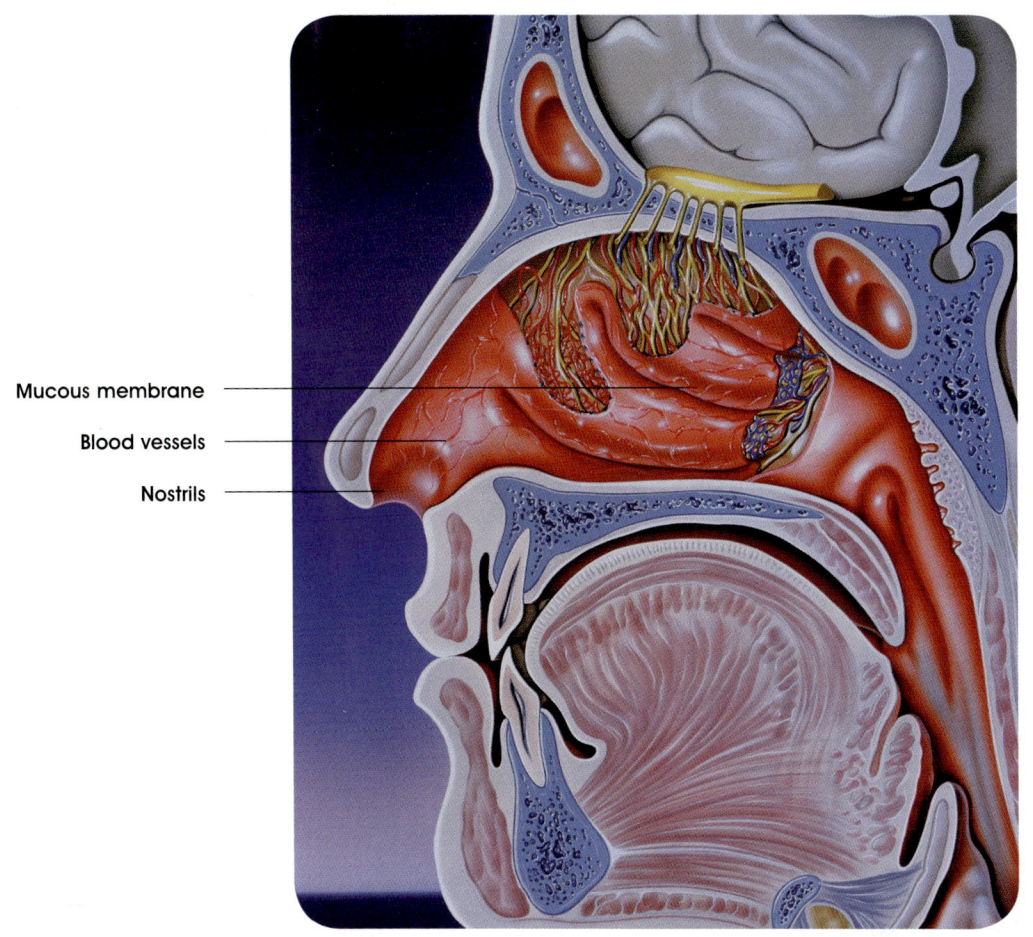

This is an illustration of the structure of a nose. Air is breathed in through the nostrils. The mucous membrane has blood vessels that when injured, result in a nosebleed.

separates your nostrils. You breathe in air through your nostrils. As you breathe, air enters both nostrils. Then it travels up the two separate passages.

Do you have a coat or jacket that has a lining? You may be surprised to learn that your nasal passages have a lining, too. They are lined with a soft, moist tissue known as a **mucous membrane**. This membrane moistens and protects the nasal passages.

Tiny, hairlike structures cover the mucous membrane that lines your nose. These structures are called cilia. The **cilia** sway back and forth. That is how they remove dust and germs from your nose.

The mucous membrane that lines your nose is filled with many tiny blood vessels. These vessels are just beneath the surface. They carry blood to the mucous membrane.

At times, an injury or scratch can break these blood vessels. The mucous membrane can become irritated as well. This often happens in cool, dry weather, when there isn't much moisture in the air. Just blowing your nose can sometimes break these blood vessels. All these things, as well as others, can lead to a nosebleed.

NOSEBLEED!

Oh, no—not again! You hear your three-year-old brother crying. You race to his room to see what's the matter.

He's sitting on the floor. Tears are flowing from his eyes. But that's not all. Blood is flowing from his nose, too.

It's not his first nosebleed. You quickly see what happened this time. Your brother was pretending to be a walrus again. The young boy stuck a plastic straw up each of his nostrils. The straws were

DID YOU KNOW?

Most nosebleeds happen when vessels near the front part of your nose tear. That's the lower part of the septum. This type of nosebleed is known as an **anterior nosebleed**. Usually, it's fairly easy to stop these nosebleeds. In most cases they can be taken care of at home. You don't need to see a doctor.

Nose picking is a common cause of nosebleeds.

supposed to be his walrus tusks. But he pushed a little too hard on one of the straws. This broke a small blood vessel in the lining of his nose. Now he is bleeding and very upset.

What happened to this boy is not uncommon. Children have been known to stick all sorts of things up their noses. It's never a good idea to do this. It can easily cause a nosebleed.

HOW NOSEBLEEDS HAPPEN

There are other common causes of nosebleeds. Sometimes people pick their noses. A sharp fingernail can break small blood vessels in the nose.

The main cause of nosebleeds, however, is a blow to the nose. Being struck in the nose by a Frisbee, for example, is usually enough to cause a nosebleed.

Being hit in the nose with a fist can give you a nosebleed, too. So try to keep a safe distance from people who punch! Nosebleeds can also occur if you fall and hit your nose.

Dry weather makes nosebleeds more likely, too. Do you live in a very dry climate? The lining of your nose can also become quite dry.

During a cold, the nose's mucous membrane can become dry. Then you are more likely to have a nosebleed.

During the winter, heated indoor air can dry out the lining of your nose as well. Having a cold or allergy can have the same effect. It isn't difficult to get a nosebleed. When the mucous membrane lining of your nose dries and cracks, the tiny blood vessels tear. The result is a nosebleed.

What To Do If It Happens To You

It's winter, and just about everybody has a cold. You've got one, too. You've been coughing all day.

You also have a runny nose. You've nearly used up a box of tissues. Your nose is red and sore. It hurts to blow it.

Then, after one big sneeze, you look down at your tissue. There's blood in it. You've got a nosebleed.

The sight of blood can be upsetting. This is especially true if it's your own. But remember, nosebleeds don't hurt. Tell yourself that you're going to be fine.

NOSEBLEED FIRST AID

If you get a nosebleed, stay calm. Try not to cry. Crying increases the blood flow to your face. This can worsen your nosebleed.

Sit down and lean forward a little. Breathe through your mouth. No matter what your friends or anyone else tells you, do not lie down. Do not tilt your head back, either. This can make the blood flow down your throat. Swallowing it can cause gagging. It can also nauseate you.

Use some tissues or a piece of gauze to absorb the blood. This will stop it from getting on your clothes or on the floor. However, don't stuff tissues or anything else up your nose. That is not the way to stop the bleeding. Instead, use your thumb and index finger to firmly squeeze your

NOSEBLEED CURES THAT DON'T WORK

You may have heard all sorts of strange ways to stop nosebleeds. These cures range from being funny to dangerous. Some date back hundreds of years.

One well known but silly cure has to do with keys. People with nosebleeds are supposed to slide a set of cold keys down their backs to stop the bleeding. Don't try it. It doesn't work. Neither does standing on one foot while repeating the words "Nosebleed, nosebleed—leave with speed."

Using a piece of soft gauze or cotton is a good way to absorb blood from a nosebleed.

nostrils together. Do this just beneath the bridge, or bony part, of your nose.

Don't stop after just a few seconds. Sit still, and keep holding your nose for at least five minutes. While you are doing this, breathe through your mouth. Applying this pressure should stop the bleeding.

If the bleeding doesn't stop, repeat what you just did. But this time, hold your nose for ten minutes. That may seem like a long time. Some people watch television or listen to music as they do this. It can make the time seem to pass more quickly.

Once the bleeding stops, take some time to rest. Try not to do anything that will start the bleeding again. Avoid playing any rough games for a while. Even if you love football, rock climbing, or skateboarding, this is not the time for it. Read a book or play a computer game instead.

Do not bend over if you can help it. Also, do not take any aspirin or **ibuprofen** while your nose is bleeding. Try not to blow your nose for a while, either. Before you know it, your nosebleed will be nothing more than a memory. Then, you'll be your old self again!

Knowing When to Get Help

You were at the playground with your best friend. You went on the swings, slide, and jungle gym. You did some rock climbing, too.

It started out as a perfect day. It didn't end that way, however. Just as you were about to go home, your friend tripped and fell. He hit his head on the steel jungle gym. When he got up, his nose was bleeding.

The playground is fun, but play with care. An injury on a piece of equipment can result in a nosebleed.

You tried to calm your friend. You read this book and knew what to do. You felt sure you could handle things.

There was a problem, though. You did everything you were supposed to do to stop a nosebleed. Yet this time, it didn't work. Your friend's nosebleed wouldn't stop.

What if this happened to you? Would you know what to do?

If a nosebleed resulting from an injury doesn't stop, get medical help right away. Also, get medical help quickly if the bleeding is unusually heavy. This is especially important if the person feels dizzy or weak. Don't try to handle this type of nosebleed on your own. Find a responsible adult to help you. If there is no adult around, dial 911 and ask for help.

WITH A DOCTOR'S HELP

A doctor can do things to stop a nosebleed that you can't. Sometimes a blood vessel needs to be **cauterized**. Heat or a medication is used to close the vessel in this procedure. This stops it from bleeding.

Other times, nasal packing is necessary. In this case the doctor packs the person's nose with a special type of gauze. This puts pressure on the blood vessel. The pressure stops the bleeding.

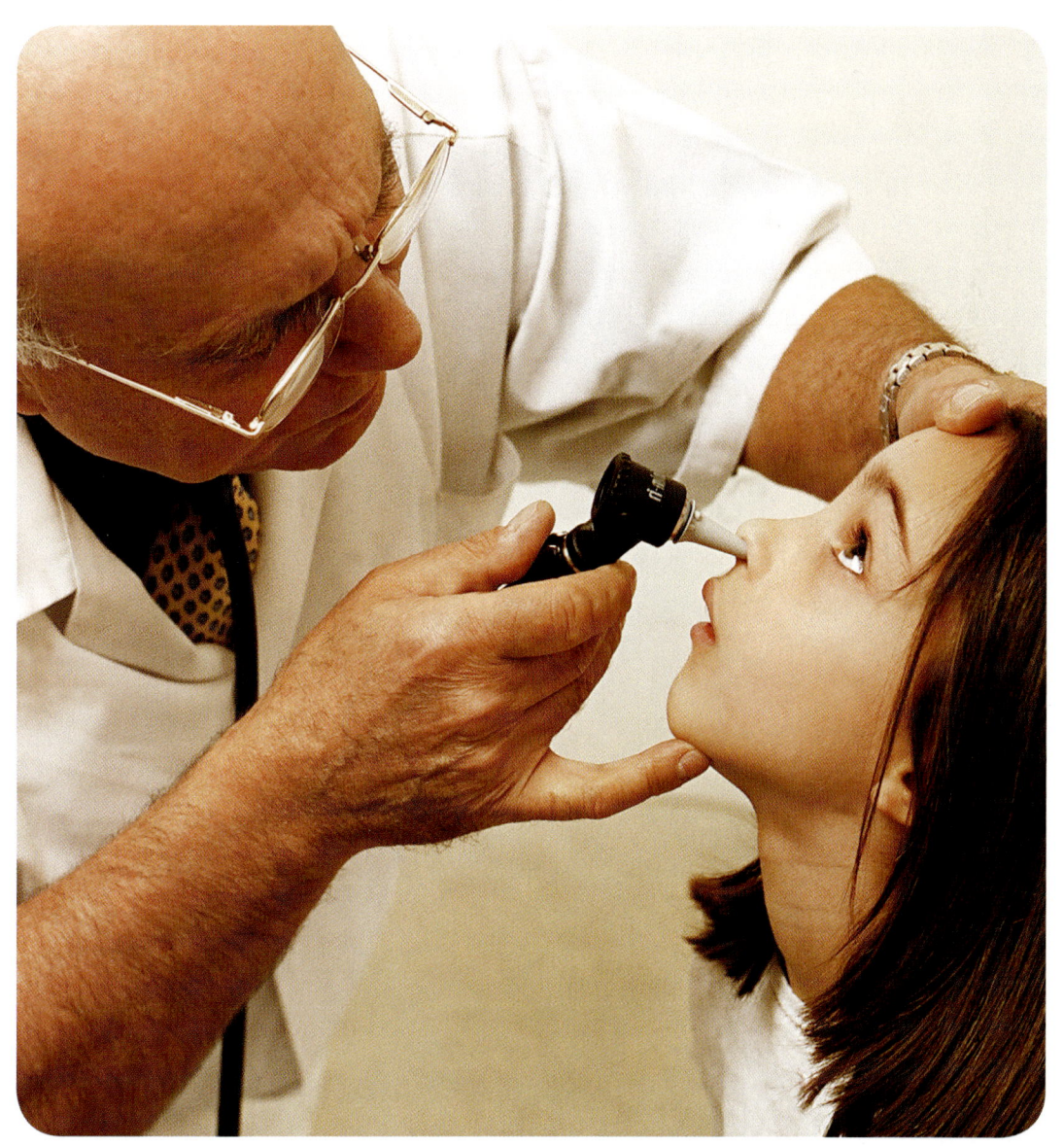

A visit to the doctor may be necessary for a severe nosebleed.

If you have a cold or allergy, don't blow your nose too hard. Blowing too hard may bring on a nosebleed.

NO MORE NOSEBLEEDS, PLEASE

There's only one thing better than stopping a nosebleed. That's not getting one to begin with. Did you know that there are things you can do to decrease your chances of getting a nosebleed?

For starters, do not pick your nose. Even if your nose feels stuffy or itchy, don't be tempted to pick it. Don't stick anything up your nose, either. What might start as a prank to make a friend laugh can end as a nosebleed.

What if you have a cold or allergy? You may need to blow your nose often. Remember not to blow too hard. Try not to rub your nose, either.

A POSTERIOR NOSEBLEED

In most cases nosebleeds are minor injuries. They are simply messy and annoying. However, at times, a nosebleed can be more serious. Some nosebleeds are harder to stop. These nosebleeds originate higher and deeper in the nose. They are known as **posterior nosebleeds**. The blood flows down the back of your mouth and throat. This happens even if you are sitting up or standing. You need to get medical attention for these nosebleeds immediately.

If the air in your house is dry, ask your parents about getting a **humidifier**. This machine adds water to the air. This can stop your nose from becoming overly dry. That makes it less likely that you'll get a nosebleed.

There are other ways to reduce nosebleeds. Putting a dab of **nasal lubricant** around the opening of your nostrils can help. This soothes any dry or irritated skin there. It can help prevent a future nosebleed.

The same is true of **saline nasal sprays**. These sprays, used two to three times a day, keep the lining of your nose moist. They also flush out dirt and pollen, which can irritate your nose.

Sometimes, nosebleeds happen when you are playing sports. It's easy to see why. Just look in the mirror. Which of the features on your face sticks out? It's your nose! That makes it more likely to be injured.

It's up to you to protect your nose. You can do that by wearing a helmet when playing football, baseball, or hockey. Nose guards protect your nose as well. These are especially important to wear when participating in sports where helmets aren't usually worn. Some people use nose guards while participating in karate, wrestling, soccer, and other sports.

When playing a sport, it's not a bad idea to protect your nose.

You can't be sure that you'll never get another nosebleed. But now you know a lot more about them. You also know what to do if you get one. That can make having a nosebleed a lot less scary.

Be sure to also use the tips in this book to help you avoid getting nosebleeds. Share them with your family and friends. The more people know about nosebleeds, the better off they'll be. That's an important step toward staying healthy and feeling good.

GLOSSARY

anterior nosebleed — a nosebleed that occurs when blood vessels near the front part of the nose rupture

cauterize — to use heat or a medication to stop a blood vessel from bleeding

cilia — the tiny, hairlike structures covering the mucous membrane (see below) of the nose

humidifier — a machine that adds moisture to the air

ibuprofen — a drug used to reduce pain, swelling, and fever

mucous membrane — the soft membrane that moistens and protects the nasal passages

nasal lubricant — a special gel that soothes dry, irritated nasal passages

posterior nosebleed — a nosebleed that occurs when blood vessels higher and deeper in the nose rupture

saline nasal spray — a spray containing salt water that keeps the lining of the nose moist

septum — the thin wall in the nose that separates the nostrils

FIND OUT MORE

BOOKS

Landau, Elaine. *Bumps, Bruises, and Scrapes.* New York: Marshall Cavendish Benchmark, 2009.

Miller, Edward. *The Monster Health Book: A Guide to Eating Healthy, Being Active & Feeling Great for Monsters & Kids!* New York: Holiday House, 2006.

Olien, Rebecca. *Smelling.* Mankato, MN: Capstone, 2005.

Woodward, Kay. *Smell.* Milwaukee, WI: Gareth Stevens Publications, 2005.

DVDS

Danger Rangers: Mission 547 Safety Rules! Educational Adventures, LLC, 2005.

Safety on Wheels with The Safety Sarge. CustomFlix, 2006.

WEB SITES

Going with the Flow of Nosebleeds

www.kidshealth.org/kid/watch/er/nosebleeds.html

A handy guide on what to do to stop a nosebleed.

Neuroscience for Kids—The Nose Knows

http://faculty.washington.edu/chudler/nosek.html

An interesting Web site that explains how our sense of smell works.

Smell—Natural History Museum of Los Angeles County

www.nhm.org/exhibitions/dogs/formfunction/smell.html

This fascinating Web site shows how dogs experience the world nose-first.

Index

activity, after a nosebleed, 18
air, dry, 10, 13–14, 24
anterior nosebleeds, 11
aspirin and ibuprofen, 18

blood vessels, **9**, 10, 11, 20
blowing your nose, **14**, 15, 18, **22**, 23
breathing, 7, 18

causes, of nosebleeds, 6, 10, 13–14
cauterizing blood vessels, 20
cilia, 10
colds and allergies, 14, 15, 23
commonness, of nosebleeds, 6
crying, nosebleeds and, 15

doctors, 20, **21**
dogs, 8, **8**
dry air, 10, 13–14, 24

elderly people, 6

face masks, 24, **25**
first aid for nosebleeds, 15–16, **17**, 18

germs, 10

help, getting, 19–20, 23–26
humidifiers, 24

ibuprofen and aspirin, 18
injuries, 5, 10, 13, 19

lying down, 16

mucus membranes, **9**, 10, 14

nasal lubricants, 24
nasal packing, 20
911, calling, 20
nose guards, 24
nose picking, **12**, 13, 23
noses, about, 7–10
nostrils, 7, 9, **9**

objects, putting in nose, 11, 13, 23
old wives tales, 16

parts, of noses, 7, **9**, 9–10
preventing nosebleeds, 23–24, **25**, 26
protection, for noses, 24, **25**

punches, nosebleeds and, 13

rescue workers, dogs and, 8
resting, after a nosebleed, 18

saline nasal sprays, 24
septum, the, 7, 9
smell, sense of, 7, 8
sports, 5, 24, **25**
stopping a nosebleed, 5–6, 15–18

throat and mouth, 16, 23
tissues, 16

what not to do for a nosebleed, 16
what to do for a nosebleed, 5–6, 15–18

young people, 6

About the Author

Award-winning author Elaine Landau has written more than three hundred books for young readers. Many of these are on health and science topics. For Marshall Cavendish, Landau has written *Asthma; Bites and Stings; Broken Bones; Bumps, Bruises, and Scrapes; Cavities and Toothaches*; and *The Common Cold* for the Head-to-Toe Health series.

Ms. Landau received her bachelor's degree in English and journalism from New York University and a master's degree in library and information science from Pratt Institute. You can visit Elaine Landau at her Web site: www.elainelandau.com.